50 Ultimate Baking Recipes

By: Kelly Johnson

Table of Contents

- Classic Chocolate Chip Cookies
- Homemade Cinnamon Rolls
- Red Velvet Cake
- Soft Pretzels
- Banana Bread
- Perfect Apple Pie
- Sourdough Bread
- Lemon Meringue Pie
- Classic Cheesecake
- Sticky Toffee Pudding
- Almond Croissants
- Blueberry Muffins
- Chocolate Fudge Brownies
- French Baguettes
- Carrot Cake with Cream Cheese Frosting
- Peanut Butter Cookies
- Flaky Biscuits
- Coconut Macaroons
- Raspberry Thumbprint Cookies
- Gingerbread Cookies
- Buttermilk Pancakes
- Pumpkin Spice Bread
- Vanilla Cupcakes with Buttercream
- Chocolate Eclairs
- Apple Galette
- Brioche Buns
- Chocolate Lava Cakes
- Shortbread Cookies
- Tiramisu
- Key Lime Pie
- Pavlova with Fresh Fruit
- Chocolate Croissants
- Raspberry Danish
- Lemon Bars
- Sugar Cookies

- Peach Cobbler
- Zucchini Bread
- Strawberry Rhubarb Pie
- Cherry Clafoutis
- Chocolate Chip Scones
- Cinnamon Sugar Donuts
- Nutella-Stuffed Crepes
- Cream Puffs
- Maple Bacon Scones
- Mocha Cake
- Bourbon Pecan Pie
- Chocolate Tart
- Flourless Chocolate Cake
- Marzipan Fruit Cake
- Baked Donuts with Glaze

Classic Chocolate Chip Cookies

Ingredients:

- 2 1/4 cups all-purpose flour
- 1/2 tsp baking soda
- 1 cup unsalted butter, softened
- 1/2 cup granulated sugar
- 1 cup packed brown sugar
- 1 tsp vanilla extract
- 2 large eggs
- 2 cups semisweet chocolate chips
- 1/2 tsp salt

Instructions:

1. Preheat your oven to 350°F (175°C). Line two baking sheets with parchment paper.
2. In a medium bowl, whisk together the flour, baking soda, and salt. Set aside.
3. In a large mixing bowl, beat the softened butter, granulated sugar, and brown sugar together with an electric mixer until light and fluffy, about 2-3 minutes.
4. Add the vanilla extract and eggs, one at a time, beating well after each addition.
5. Gradually add the dry ingredients to the wet ingredients, mixing just until combined.
6. Stir in the chocolate chips with a spatula or spoon.
7. Drop rounded tablespoonfuls of dough onto the prepared baking sheets, spacing them about 2 inches apart.
8. Bake for 10-12 minutes or until the edges are golden but the centers are still soft.
9. Let the cookies cool on the baking sheets for a few minutes before transferring them to wire racks to cool completely.

Homemade Cinnamon Rolls
Ingredients:

- 2 1/4 cups all-purpose flour
- 1/4 cup granulated sugar
- 1 tsp active dry yeast
- 1/2 tsp salt
- 1/2 cup whole milk, warmed
- 1/4 cup unsalted butter, melted
- 1 large egg
- 1 tsp vanilla extract
- 1/2 cup packed brown sugar
- 1 tbsp ground cinnamon
- 1/4 cup unsalted butter, softened

Instructions:

1. In a bowl, combine 1 cup of flour, sugar, yeast, and salt. In a separate bowl, mix the warm milk, melted butter, egg, and vanilla.
2. Add the wet ingredients to the dry ingredients and stir until combined. Gradually add the remaining flour, mixing until a dough forms.
3. Knead the dough for 5-7 minutes until smooth and elastic. Place in a greased bowl, cover, and let it rise for 1 hour.
4. Roll out the dough into a rectangle, then spread softened butter, sprinkle with cinnamon, and brown sugar.
5. Roll up the dough, slice into rolls, and place in a greased baking dish. Let them rise for 30 minutes.
6. Preheat the oven to 350°F (175°C) and bake the rolls for 20-25 minutes until golden brown.
7. Drizzle with icing made from powdered sugar, milk, and vanilla.

Red Velvet Cake
Ingredients:

- 2 1/2 cups all-purpose flour
- 1 1/2 cups granulated sugar
- 1 tsp baking soda
- 1 tsp cocoa powder
- 1/2 tsp salt
- 1 1/2 cups vegetable oil
- 1 cup buttermilk
- 2 large eggs
- 2 tbsp red food coloring
- 1 tsp vanilla extract
- 1 tsp white vinegar
- 8 oz cream cheese, softened
- 1/4 cup unsalted butter, softened
- 4 cups powdered sugar

Instructions:

1. Preheat the oven to 350°F (175°C). Grease and flour two 9-inch round cake pans.
2. In a bowl, combine the flour, sugar, baking soda, cocoa powder, and salt. In a separate bowl, mix oil, buttermilk, eggs, food coloring, vanilla, and vinegar.
3. Gradually add the wet ingredients to the dry ingredients and mix until smooth.
4. Divide the batter between the cake pans and bake for 30-35 minutes until a toothpick comes out clean.
5. Let the cakes cool before frosting with cream cheese frosting.
6. For the frosting, beat the cream cheese and butter, then add powdered sugar until smooth. Frost the cooled cakes.

Soft Pretzels
Ingredients:

- 2 1/4 cups all-purpose flour
- 1 tsp salt
- 1 tbsp granulated sugar
- 1 tbsp active dry yeast
- 3/4 cup warm water
- 2 tbsp unsalted butter, melted
- 8 cups water (for boiling)
- 1/4 cup baking soda
- Coarse salt (for topping)

Instructions:

1. In a bowl, combine flour, salt, and sugar. Dissolve yeast in warm water, then add to the dry ingredients with melted butter. Stir to form a dough.
2. Knead the dough on a floured surface for 5-7 minutes, then let it rise for 1 hour, covered.
3. Preheat the oven to 450°F (230°C). Bring 8 cups of water and baking soda to a boil in a large pot.
4. Punch down the dough, divide into 8 portions, and roll each into a long rope. Shape into a pretzel and carefully drop into boiling water for 30 seconds per pretzel.
5. Place pretzels on a baking sheet and sprinkle with coarse salt. Bake for 12-15 minutes until golden brown.
6. Let cool slightly before serving.

Banana Bread

Ingredients:

- 2-3 ripe bananas, mashed
- 1/2 cup unsalted butter, melted
- 1 cup granulated sugar
- 2 eggs
- 1 tsp vanilla extract
- 2 cups all-purpose flour
- 1 tsp baking soda
- 1/4 tsp salt
- 1/2 cup buttermilk

Instructions:

1. Preheat the oven to 350°F (175°C). Grease a loaf pan.
2. In a bowl, combine mashed bananas, melted butter, sugar, eggs, and vanilla.
3. In a separate bowl, whisk together flour, baking soda, and salt.
4. Gradually add the dry ingredients to the wet ingredients, alternating with buttermilk.
5. Pour the batter into the prepared pan and bake for 60-65 minutes, or until a toothpick comes out clean.
6. Let cool before slicing and serving.

Perfect Apple Pie
Ingredients:

- 6-8 medium apples, peeled and sliced
- 1 tbsp lemon juice
- 3/4 cup granulated sugar
- 1/4 cup packed brown sugar
- 1 tsp ground cinnamon
- 1/4 tsp ground nutmeg
- 2 tbsp all-purpose flour
- 1 tbsp cornstarch
- 1/4 tsp salt
- 1 tbsp butter
- 1 package refrigerated pie crusts

Instructions:

1. Preheat the oven to 425°F (220°C).
2. Toss the apples with lemon juice, sugars, cinnamon, nutmeg, flour, cornstarch, and salt.
3. Roll out one pie crust and line a pie dish. Add the apple mixture and dot with butter.
4. Top with the second pie crust, crimp edges, and cut slits in the top for ventilation.
5. Bake for 45-50 minutes, or until the crust is golden brown and the filling is bubbling.
6. Let cool before serving.

Sourdough Bread
Ingredients:

- 1 cup sourdough starter
- 1 1/2 cups warm water
- 3 cups all-purpose flour
- 1 tbsp sugar
- 1 tsp salt

Instructions:

1. In a bowl, mix the sourdough starter with warm water, sugar, and salt.
2. Gradually add the flour, kneading until smooth.
3. Cover and let the dough rise for 2-3 hours, or until doubled in size.
4. Preheat the oven to 450°F (230°C).
5. Shape the dough into a loaf, place it in a greased pan, and let it rise for another 30 minutes.
6. Bake for 35-40 minutes, until the bread sounds hollow when tapped. Let cool before slicing.

Lemon Meringue Pie
Ingredients:

- 1 pie crust, baked
- 1 1/2 cups granulated sugar
- 1/4 cup cornstarch
- 1/4 tsp salt
- 1 1/2 cups water
- 3 large egg yolks, beaten
- 2 tbsp unsalted butter
- 1/2 cup freshly squeezed lemon juice
- 1 tbsp lemon zest
- 3 large egg whites
- 1/4 tsp cream of tartar
- 1/4 cup granulated sugar (for meringue)

Instructions:

1. Preheat the oven to 350°F (175°C).
2. In a saucepan, combine sugar, cornstarch, salt, and water. Cook over medium heat until thickened.
3. Slowly add the beaten egg yolks, then cook for another 2-3 minutes. Remove from heat and stir in butter, lemon juice, and zest.
4. Pour the filling into the baked pie crust.
5. In a bowl, beat the egg whites with cream of tartar until stiff peaks form. Gradually add sugar and continue beating.
6. Spread the meringue over the lemon filling, sealing the edges.
7. Bake for 10-15 minutes until the meringue is golden brown. Let cool before serving.

Classic Cheesecake
Ingredients:

- 1 1/2 cups graham cracker crumbs
- 1/4 cup granulated sugar
- 1/2 cup unsalted butter, melted
- 4 packages (8 oz each) cream cheese, softened
- 1 cup granulated sugar
- 1 tsp vanilla extract
- 4 large eggs
- 1 cup sour cream

Instructions:

1. Preheat the oven to 325°F (160°C).
2. Combine graham cracker crumbs, sugar, and melted butter. Press into the bottom of a springform pan.
3. Beat cream cheese, sugar, and vanilla until smooth. Add eggs one at a time, mixing well after each addition.
4. Pour the mixture over the crust and bake for 45-50 minutes, or until set.
5. Let cool, then chill in the refrigerator for at least 4 hours.
6. Before serving, top with sour cream.

Sticky Toffee Pudding
Ingredients:

- 1 cup all-purpose flour
- 1 tsp baking powder
- 1/4 tsp salt
- 1/2 cup unsalted butter, softened
- 1 cup packed brown sugar
- 2 large eggs
- 1 tsp vanilla extract
- 1/2 cup finely chopped dates
- 1/2 cup boiling water

Instructions:

1. Preheat the oven to 350°F (175°C). Grease a baking dish.
2. In a bowl, combine flour, baking powder, and salt.
3. In another bowl, cream the butter and brown sugar. Add eggs and vanilla, and beat until smooth.
4. Stir in the flour mixture and chopped dates. Gradually add the boiling water.
5. Pour the batter into the prepared dish and bake for 30-35 minutes, until set.
6. For the sauce, combine 1/2 cup heavy cream, 1/2 cup brown sugar, and 1/4 cup butter in a saucepan. Simmer until thickened.
7. Serve the pudding warm with the toffee sauce poured over it.

Almond Croissants
Ingredients:

- 2 cups all-purpose flour
- 1/4 tsp salt
- 1 tbsp granulated sugar
- 1 tsp instant yeast
- 3/4 cup warm water
- 2 tbsp unsalted butter, melted
- 1 egg, beaten
- 1/2 cup almond paste
- 1/4 cup powdered sugar
- 1 tbsp heavy cream

Instructions:

1. In a bowl, mix flour, salt, sugar, and yeast. Add warm water, melted butter, and egg.
2. Knead the dough until smooth, then cover and let rise for 1 hour.
3. Roll out the dough and fold in almond paste.
4. Shape the dough into croissants and bake at 375°F (190°C) for 15-20 minutes.
5. Drizzle with a glaze made from powdered sugar and cream.

Blueberry Muffins
Ingredients:

- 2 cups all-purpose flour
- 3/4 cup granulated sugar
- 1/2 tsp salt
- 2 tsp baking powder
- 1/2 tsp baking soda
- 1/2 cup unsalted butter, melted
- 2 large eggs
- 1 cup buttermilk
- 1 tsp vanilla extract
- 1 1/2 cups fresh blueberries

Instructions:

1. Preheat the oven to 375°F (190°C). Grease a muffin tin.
2. In a bowl, mix flour, sugar, salt, baking powder, and baking soda.
3. In another bowl, whisk melted butter, eggs, buttermilk, and vanilla.
4. Add the wet ingredients to the dry ingredients and fold in blueberries.
5. Divide the batter between the muffin cups and bake for 20-25 minutes, or until golden brown.
6. Let cool slightly before serving.

Chocolate Fudge Brownies
Ingredients:

- 1 cup unsalted butter, melted
- 1 cup granulated sugar
- 1 cup packed brown sugar
- 4 large eggs
- 1 tsp vanilla extract
- 1 cup all-purpose flour
- 1/2 cup unsweetened cocoa powder
- 1/4 tsp salt
- 1/2 tsp baking powder
- 1 cup semi-sweet chocolate chips

Instructions:

1. Preheat the oven to 350°F (175°C). Grease a 9x13-inch baking pan.
2. In a large bowl, mix the melted butter, granulated sugar, and brown sugar. Add eggs and vanilla, and mix until smooth.
3. Sift together the flour, cocoa powder, salt, and baking powder, then fold into the wet ingredients.
4. Stir in the chocolate chips.
5. Pour the batter into the prepared pan and bake for 30-35 minutes, or until a toothpick inserted comes out clean.
6. Let cool before cutting into squares.

French Baguettes
Ingredients:

- 3 cups all-purpose flour
- 1 1/2 tsp salt
- 1 tsp instant yeast
- 1 1/4 cups warm water
- 1 tbsp olive oil

Instructions:

1. In a bowl, combine flour, salt, and yeast. Add warm water and olive oil, and stir to form a dough.
2. Knead the dough for 10 minutes until smooth, then cover and let rise for 1 hour.
3. Preheat the oven to 475°F (245°C) and place a baking stone or sheet in the oven.
4. Punch down the dough, divide it into two pieces, and shape into baguettes.
5. Place the baguettes on a parchment-lined baking sheet and let rise for 30 minutes.
6. Score the tops with a sharp knife and bake for 20-25 minutes until golden brown.

Carrot Cake with Cream Cheese Frosting
Ingredients:

- 2 cups all-purpose flour
- 1 1/2 tsp baking powder
- 1 tsp baking soda
- 1 1/2 tsp ground cinnamon
- 1/2 tsp ground nutmeg
- 1/4 tsp salt
- 4 large eggs
- 1 1/2 cups vegetable oil
- 1 1/2 cups granulated sugar
- 1 cup packed brown sugar
- 2 tsp vanilla extract
- 3 cups grated carrots
- 1 cup chopped walnuts (optional)
- 8 oz cream cheese, softened
- 1/2 cup unsalted butter, softened
- 4 cups powdered sugar
- 1 tsp vanilla extract

Instructions:

1. Preheat the oven to 350°F (175°C). Grease and flour two 9-inch round cake pans.
2. In a bowl, combine flour, baking powder, baking soda, cinnamon, nutmeg, and salt.
3. In another bowl, whisk eggs, oil, granulated sugar, brown sugar, and vanilla. Add the dry ingredients and mix until smooth.
4. Stir in the grated carrots and walnuts.
5. Divide the batter evenly between the pans and bake for 30-35 minutes, or until a toothpick comes out clean.
6. Let the cakes cool completely before frosting.
7. For the frosting, beat cream cheese and butter until smooth. Gradually add powdered sugar and vanilla, and beat until fluffy.
8. Frost the cooled cakes and serve.

Peanut Butter Cookies
Ingredients:

- 1 cup unsalted peanut butter
- 1 cup granulated sugar
- 1 large egg
- 1 tsp vanilla extract

Instructions:

1. Preheat the oven to 350°F (175°C). Grease a baking sheet.
2. In a bowl, mix peanut butter, sugar, egg, and vanilla until smooth.
3. Roll the dough into balls and place them on the prepared sheet. Flatten with a fork in a crisscross pattern.
4. Bake for 8-10 minutes until the edges are golden brown.
5. Let cool on a wire rack.

Flaky Biscuits
Ingredients:

- 2 cups all-purpose flour
- 1 tbsp baking powder
- 1/2 tsp salt
- 1/2 tsp baking soda
- 1/4 cup unsalted butter, chilled
- 3/4 cup buttermilk

Instructions:

1. Preheat the oven to 450°F (230°C). Grease a baking sheet.
2. In a bowl, whisk together flour, baking powder, salt, and baking soda.
3. Cut the butter into small pieces and work it into the flour mixture using a pastry cutter or your fingers until the mixture resembles coarse crumbs.
4. Gradually add the buttermilk and stir until just combined.
5. Turn the dough out onto a floured surface and gently knead a few times. Roll the dough to 1-inch thickness and cut into rounds.
6. Place the biscuits on the baking sheet and bake for 10-12 minutes until golden brown.

Coconut Macaroons
Ingredients:

- 2 1/2 cups sweetened shredded coconut
- 2/3 cup granulated sugar
- 1/4 tsp salt
- 2 large egg whites
- 1 tsp vanilla extract

Instructions:

1. Preheat the oven to 325°F (160°C). Grease a baking sheet.
2. In a bowl, combine coconut, sugar, and salt.
3. In another bowl, beat egg whites and vanilla until stiff peaks form.
4. Gently fold the egg whites into the coconut mixture.
5. Drop spoonfuls of the mixture onto the prepared sheet.
6. Bake for 15-20 minutes, until golden brown. Let cool before serving.

Raspberry Thumbprint Cookies
Ingredients:

- 1 cup unsalted butter, softened
- 1/2 cup granulated sugar
- 1 tsp vanilla extract
- 2 cups all-purpose flour
- 1/4 tsp salt
- 1/2 cup raspberry jam

Instructions:

1. Preheat the oven to 350°F (175°C). Grease a baking sheet.
2. In a bowl, cream together butter, sugar, and vanilla. Gradually add flour and salt, mixing until dough forms.
3. Roll the dough into 1-inch balls and place on the prepared sheet. Press a thumbprint into the center of each cookie.
4. Fill each thumbprint with a small amount of raspberry jam.
5. Bake for 10-12 minutes, or until the edges are lightly golden. Let cool before serving.

Gingerbread Cookies
Ingredients:

- 3 cups all-purpose flour
- 1 tsp baking soda
- 1 tbsp ground ginger
- 1 tsp ground cinnamon
- 1/2 tsp ground cloves
- 1/4 tsp salt
- 1/2 cup unsalted butter, softened
- 1/2 cup brown sugar, packed
- 1 large egg
- 1/2 cup molasses
- 1 tsp vanilla extract

Instructions:

1. Preheat the oven to 350°F (175°C). Grease a baking sheet.
2. In a bowl, whisk together flour, baking soda, ginger, cinnamon, cloves, and salt.
3. In another bowl, cream together butter and brown sugar. Add the egg, molasses, and vanilla, and mix well.
4. Gradually add the dry ingredients to the wet mixture, stirring until dough forms.
5. Roll the dough out on a floured surface and cut into shapes using cookie cutters.
6. Place the cookies on the baking sheet and bake for 8-10 minutes. Let cool before decorating.

Buttermilk Pancakes
Ingredients:

- 1 1/2 cups all-purpose flour
- 1 tbsp baking powder
- 1/2 tsp baking soda
- 1/2 tsp salt
- 1 1/2 cups buttermilk
- 2 large eggs
- 2 tbsp unsalted butter, melted
- 1 tbsp sugar
- 1 tsp vanilla extract

Instructions:

1. Preheat a griddle or skillet over medium heat and lightly grease with butter.
2. In a bowl, whisk together flour, baking powder, baking soda, salt, and sugar.
3. In a separate bowl, mix together buttermilk, eggs, melted butter, and vanilla.
4. Add the wet ingredients to the dry ingredients and stir until just combined (don't overmix).
5. Pour 1/4 cup of batter onto the griddle for each pancake. Cook for 2-3 minutes per side until golden brown.
6. Serve with syrup, butter, and your favorite toppings.

Pumpkin Spice Bread
Ingredients:

- 1 3/4 cups all-purpose flour
- 1 1/2 tsp baking soda
- 1 tsp ground cinnamon
- 1/2 tsp ground nutmeg
- 1/4 tsp ground ginger
- 1/4 tsp salt
- 1/2 cup unsalted butter, softened
- 1 cup granulated sugar
- 2 large eggs
- 1 cup canned pumpkin puree
- 1 tsp vanilla extract
- 1/2 cup buttermilk

Instructions:

1. Preheat the oven to 350°F (175°C) and grease a loaf pan.
2. In a bowl, whisk together flour, baking soda, cinnamon, nutmeg, ginger, and salt.
3. In a separate bowl, cream together butter and sugar until light and fluffy. Add eggs, one at a time, beating well after each addition.
4. Stir in pumpkin and vanilla, then gradually add the dry ingredients, alternating with the buttermilk.
5. Pour the batter into the prepared pan and smooth the top.
6. Bake for 60-70 minutes, or until a toothpick comes out clean. Let cool before slicing.

Vanilla Cupcakes with Buttercream
Ingredients:

- 1 1/2 cups all-purpose flour
- 1 1/2 tsp baking powder
- 1/2 tsp salt
- 1/2 cup unsalted butter, softened
- 1 cup granulated sugar
- 2 large eggs
- 2 tsp vanilla extract
- 1/2 cup milk

Buttercream Frosting:

- 1 cup unsalted butter, softened
- 3-4 cups powdered sugar
- 1 tsp vanilla extract
- 2-3 tbsp heavy cream

Instructions:

1. Preheat the oven to 350°F (175°C) and line a muffin tin with paper liners.
2. In a bowl, whisk together flour, baking powder, and salt.
3. In a separate bowl, cream together butter and sugar until light and fluffy. Add eggs, one at a time, and vanilla, mixing well.
4. Gradually add the dry ingredients, alternating with milk, and mix until just combined.
5. Divide the batter among the muffin cups, filling each about 2/3 full.
6. Bake for 18-20 minutes, or until a toothpick comes out clean. Let cool.
7. For the frosting, beat butter until smooth. Gradually add powdered sugar and vanilla, then add heavy cream to reach the desired consistency.
8. Frost the cooled cupcakes and enjoy!

Chocolate Eclairs
Ingredients:

- 1 cup water
- 1/2 cup unsalted butter
- 1 cup all-purpose flour
- 1/4 tsp salt
- 4 large eggs
- 1 cup heavy cream
- 1 tsp vanilla extract
- 4 oz semi-sweet chocolate, chopped
- 1 tbsp unsalted butter

Instructions:

1. Preheat the oven to 400°F (200°C) and line a baking sheet with parchment paper.
2. In a saucepan, bring water and butter to a boil. Stir in flour and salt until the dough forms a ball. Remove from heat and cool for a few minutes.
3. Add eggs, one at a time, beating after each addition until smooth.
4. Transfer the dough to a piping bag and pipe 4-inch-long strips onto the baking sheet.
5. Bake for 25-30 minutes, or until golden brown and puffed. Cool completely.
6. For the filling, whip heavy cream with vanilla until stiff peaks form.
7. For the chocolate glaze, melt chocolate and butter in a heatproof bowl over simmering water.
8. Slice the cooled eclairs in half, fill with whipped cream, and dip the tops in the chocolate glaze. Serve immediately.

Apple Galette
Ingredients:

- 1 pie crust (store-bought or homemade)
- 4-5 medium apples, peeled, cored, and sliced
- 1/4 cup granulated sugar
- 1 tbsp all-purpose flour
- 1 tsp ground cinnamon
- 1 tbsp lemon juice
- 1 tbsp butter, cubed
- 1 egg (for egg wash)

Instructions:

1. Preheat the oven to 375°F (190°C) and line a baking sheet with parchment paper.
2. Roll out the pie crust on a floured surface to about 12 inches in diameter.
3. In a bowl, toss the apple slices with sugar, flour, cinnamon, and lemon juice.
4. Arrange the apples in the center of the pie crust, leaving a border around the edges.
5. Dot the apples with butter and fold the edges of the crust over the apples.
6. Brush the crust with beaten egg.
7. Bake for 40-45 minutes, or until the crust is golden brown and the apples are tender. Let cool before serving.

Brioche Buns
Ingredients:

- 1/2 cup warm milk
- 2 1/4 tsp active dry yeast
- 1/4 cup granulated sugar
- 2 cups all-purpose flour
- 1/4 tsp salt
- 1/2 cup unsalted butter, softened
- 2 large eggs
- 1 egg yolk (for egg wash)

Instructions:

1. In a bowl, combine warm milk, yeast, and sugar. Let sit for 5 minutes to activate the yeast.
2. In a separate bowl, combine flour and salt. Add the yeast mixture, butter, and eggs, and mix until smooth.
3. Knead the dough for 10 minutes until elastic. Cover and let rise for 1 hour.
4. Punch down the dough and divide it into 8 equal portions. Shape each into a bun and place on a greased baking sheet.
5. Let rise for another 30 minutes.
6. Preheat the oven to 375°F (190°C) and brush the buns with egg yolk.
7. Bake for 15-20 minutes, or until golden brown. Let cool before serving.

Chocolate Lava Cakes
Ingredients:

- 1/2 cup unsalted butter
- 4 oz semi-sweet chocolate, chopped
- 1 cup powdered sugar
- 2 large eggs
- 2 egg yolks
- 1 tsp vanilla extract
- 1/4 cup all-purpose flour

Instructions:

1. Preheat the oven to 425°F (220°C) and grease 4 ramekins.
2. Melt butter and chocolate together in a heatproof bowl over simmering water.
3. Whisk in powdered sugar, then add eggs, egg yolks, and vanilla, whisking until smooth.
4. Fold in flour.
5. Pour the batter into the prepared ramekins, filling them about 2/3 full.
6. Bake for 12-14 minutes, or until the edges are set but the center is soft.
7. Let cool for 1 minute, then invert onto plates and serve.

Shortbread Cookies
Ingredients:

- 1 cup unsalted butter, softened
- 1/2 cup granulated sugar
- 2 cups all-purpose flour
- 1/4 tsp salt

Instructions:

1. Preheat the oven to 350°F (175°C) and line a baking sheet with parchment paper.
2. Beat butter and sugar until creamy.
3. Gradually add flour and salt, mixing until the dough comes together.
4. Roll the dough out to 1/4-inch thickness and cut into shapes with cookie cutters.
5. Place on the prepared baking sheet and bake for 12-15 minutes, or until lightly golden. Let cool before serving.

Tiramisu
Ingredients:

- 1 1/2 cups heavy cream
- 1/2 cup mascarpone cheese
- 1/2 cup powdered sugar
- 1 tsp vanilla extract
- 1 cup brewed coffee, cooled
- 1 tbsp coffee liqueur (optional)
- 2 tbsp cocoa powder
- 24-30 ladyfinger cookies
- Dark chocolate shavings (for garnish)

Instructions:

1. In a large bowl, whisk the heavy cream, mascarpone, powdered sugar, and vanilla until stiff peaks form.
2. In a shallow dish, combine the brewed coffee and coffee liqueur.
3. Dip the ladyfingers into the coffee mixture one at a time and layer them at the bottom of a serving dish.
4. Spread half of the mascarpone mixture over the ladyfingers. Repeat with another layer of dipped ladyfingers and remaining mascarpone mixture.
5. Refrigerate for at least 4 hours, or overnight.
6. Before serving, dust with cocoa powder and garnish with chocolate shavings.

Key Lime Pie
Ingredients:

- 1 1/2 cups graham cracker crumbs
- 1/4 cup sugar
- 1/2 cup unsalted butter, melted
- 1 can (14 oz) sweetened condensed milk
- 1/2 cup fresh key lime juice
- 3 large egg yolks
- 1/2 tsp vanilla extract
- Whipped cream (for topping)

Instructions:

1. Preheat the oven to 350°F (175°C).
2. Mix the graham cracker crumbs, sugar, and melted butter in a bowl. Press the mixture into the bottom of a pie pan to form a crust.
3. Bake the crust for 8-10 minutes until golden brown, then let it cool.
4. In a separate bowl, whisk together the condensed milk, key lime juice, egg yolks, and vanilla.
5. Pour the mixture into the cooled crust and bake for 15-18 minutes.
6. Let the pie cool, then refrigerate for at least 2 hours before serving. Top with whipped cream before serving.

Pavlova with Fresh Fruit
Ingredients:

- 4 large egg whites
- 1 cup granulated sugar
- 1 tsp vanilla extract
- 1 tsp white vinegar
- 1 tbsp cornstarch
- 1 cup heavy cream
- Fresh fruit (such as kiwi, berries, or passionfruit)

Instructions:

1. Preheat the oven to 250°F (120°C) and line a baking sheet with parchment paper.
2. Whisk the egg whites in a bowl until soft peaks form. Gradually add the sugar, 1 tbsp at a time, until the meringue is glossy and stiff peaks form.
3. Fold in the vanilla, vinegar, and cornstarch.
4. Spoon the meringue onto the prepared baking sheet, shaping it into a round disk with raised edges.
5. Bake for 1 hour, then turn off the oven and let the meringue cool inside with the door slightly ajar.
6. Whip the heavy cream until stiff peaks form, then spoon it on top of the cooled pavlova.
7. Top with fresh fruit and serve immediately.

Chocolate Croissants
Ingredients:

- 1 package puff pastry sheets (store-bought)
- 4 oz semi-sweet chocolate, chopped
- 1 egg (for egg wash)
- Powdered sugar (for garnish)

Instructions:

1. Preheat the oven to 400°F (200°C) and line a baking sheet with parchment paper.
2. Roll out the puff pastry sheets and cut into triangles.
3. Place a few pieces of chocolate in the center of each triangle.
4. Roll the pastry up from the wide end, forming croissants.
5. Brush the tops with the beaten egg and bake for 15-20 minutes, or until golden brown.
6. Once cooled, dust with powdered sugar and serve.

Raspberry Danish
Ingredients:

- 1 sheet puff pastry
- 1/2 cup raspberry jam
- 1 egg (for egg wash)
- Powdered sugar (for garnish)

Instructions:

1. Preheat the oven to 375°F (190°C) and line a baking sheet with parchment paper.
2. Roll out the puff pastry and cut into squares.
3. Spoon a small amount of raspberry jam into the center of each square.
4. Fold the corners of the pastry to the center, pinching them to form a pocket.
5. Brush the top with beaten egg and bake for 15-20 minutes.
6. Once baked, dust with powdered sugar and serve.

Lemon Bars
Ingredients:

- 1 1/2 cups all-purpose flour
- 1/4 cup powdered sugar
- 1/2 cup unsalted butter, softened
- 3 large eggs
- 1 cup granulated sugar
- 2 tbsp all-purpose flour
- 1/2 tsp baking powder
- 1/4 cup fresh lemon juice
- Powdered sugar (for dusting)

Instructions:

1. Preheat the oven to 350°F (175°C) and grease a 9x9-inch baking pan.
2. In a bowl, combine 1 1/2 cups flour and powdered sugar, then cut in butter until crumbly. Press the mixture into the bottom of the prepared pan.
3. Bake the crust for 15-20 minutes, until lightly golden.
4. In another bowl, whisk together eggs, granulated sugar, 2 tbsp flour, baking powder, and lemon juice.
5. Pour the lemon mixture over the baked crust and bake for an additional 20-25 minutes.
6. Let cool before slicing and dusting with powdered sugar.

Sugar Cookies
Ingredients:

- 2 3/4 cups all-purpose flour
- 1 tsp baking soda
- 1 tsp cream of tartar
- 1 cup unsalted butter, softened
- 1 1/2 cups granulated sugar
- 2 large eggs
- 1 tsp vanilla extract
- Additional sugar (for rolling)

Instructions:

1. Preheat the oven to 350°F (175°C) and line a baking sheet with parchment paper.
2. In a bowl, whisk together flour, baking soda, and cream of tartar.
3. In a separate bowl, cream together butter and sugar. Add eggs and vanilla, mixing well.
4. Gradually add the dry ingredients to the butter mixture.
5. Roll the dough into small balls and dip in sugar. Place them on the prepared baking sheet.
6. Bake for 8-10 minutes, or until the edges are lightly golden. Let cool before serving.

Peach Cobbler
Ingredients:

- 4 cups fresh or frozen peaches, sliced
- 1 cup granulated sugar
- 1 tbsp lemon juice
- 1 tsp vanilla extract
- 1 1/2 cups all-purpose flour
- 1 tbsp baking powder
- 1/4 tsp salt
- 1/4 cup unsalted butter, melted
- 3/4 cup milk
- 1/2 tsp ground cinnamon

Instructions:

1. Preheat the oven to 375°F (190°C) and grease a 9x9-inch baking dish.
2. In a bowl, combine the peaches, sugar, lemon juice, and vanilla. Pour into the prepared baking dish.
3. In another bowl, whisk together flour, baking powder, salt, and cinnamon. Stir in the melted butter and milk until smooth.
4. Pour the batter over the peaches and spread evenly.
5. Bake for 35-40 minutes, or until the top is golden brown and the filling is bubbly. Let cool slightly before serving.

Zucchini Bread
Ingredients:

- 2 cups all-purpose flour
- 1 tsp baking soda
- 1/2 tsp baking powder
- 1/2 tsp salt
- 1 tsp ground cinnamon
- 1/2 tsp ground nutmeg
- 3/4 cup vegetable oil
- 2 large eggs
- 1 1/2 cups granulated sugar
- 1 tsp vanilla extract
- 2 cups grated zucchini (about 2 medium zucchinis)
- 1/2 cup chopped walnuts or pecans (optional)

Instructions:

1. Preheat the oven to 350°F (175°C). Grease and flour a 9x5-inch loaf pan.
2. In a large bowl, whisk together the flour, baking soda, baking powder, salt, cinnamon, and nutmeg.
3. In another bowl, whisk together the oil, eggs, sugar, and vanilla until smooth.
4. Stir in the grated zucchini and fold in the dry ingredients until combined.
5. Pour the batter into the prepared pan and sprinkle with nuts, if using.
6. Bake for 55-60 minutes, or until a toothpick inserted in the center comes out clean.
7. Let the bread cool in the pan for 10 minutes before transferring to a wire rack to cool completely.

Strawberry Rhubarb Pie
Ingredients:

- 2 cups fresh strawberries, hulled and sliced
- 2 cups chopped rhubarb
- 1 1/2 cups granulated sugar
- 2 tbsp cornstarch
- 1 tbsp lemon juice
- 1/4 tsp salt
- 1 tbsp butter, cut into small pieces
- 1 package refrigerated pie crusts

Instructions:

1. Preheat the oven to 375°F (190°C).
2. Roll out one pie crust and fit it into a 9-inch pie dish.
3. In a large bowl, combine the strawberries, rhubarb, sugar, cornstarch, lemon juice, and salt. Stir to combine.
4. Pour the fruit mixture into the prepared pie crust and dot with butter.
5. Roll out the second pie crust and place it over the filling. Crimp the edges and cut slits in the top to allow steam to escape.
6. Bake for 45-50 minutes, or until the crust is golden and the filling is bubbling.
7. Let the pie cool before serving.

Cherry Clafoutis
Ingredients:

- 2 cups fresh or frozen cherries, pitted
- 1/2 cup granulated sugar
- 1 tsp vanilla extract
- 1/4 tsp almond extract (optional)
- 3 large eggs
- 1/2 cup milk
- 1/2 cup all-purpose flour
- 1/4 tsp salt
- Powdered sugar (for dusting)

Instructions:

1. Preheat the oven to 375°F (190°C) and grease a 9-inch round or oval baking dish.
2. Arrange the cherries in the bottom of the dish.
3. In a bowl, whisk together the eggs, milk, sugar, vanilla, almond extract, flour, and salt until smooth.
4. Pour the batter over the cherries and bake for 40-45 minutes, or until puffed and golden.
5. Let the clafoutis cool slightly before dusting with powdered sugar and serving.

Chocolate Chip Scones

Ingredients:

- 2 cups all-purpose flour
- 1/4 cup granulated sugar
- 1 tbsp baking powder
- 1/2 tsp salt
- 1/2 cup cold unsalted butter, cubed
- 1/2 cup chocolate chips
- 1/2 cup heavy cream
- 1 large egg
- 1 tsp vanilla extract
- 1 tbsp milk (for brushing)

Instructions:

1. Preheat the oven to 400°F (200°C) and line a baking sheet with parchment paper.
2. In a large bowl, whisk together the flour, sugar, baking powder, and salt.
3. Cut in the cold butter using a pastry cutter or your hands until the mixture resembles coarse crumbs.
4. Stir in the chocolate chips.
5. In a separate bowl, whisk together the cream, egg, and vanilla. Add the wet ingredients to the dry ingredients and stir until just combined.
6. Turn the dough onto a floured surface and gently knead until it comes together. Pat it into a circle about 1 inch thick.
7. Cut the dough into 8 wedges and place them on the prepared baking sheet. Brush with milk.
8. Bake for 15-18 minutes, or until golden brown. Let cool slightly before serving.

Cinnamon Sugar Donuts
Ingredients:

- 1 1/2 cups all-purpose flour
- 1/2 cup granulated sugar
- 1 1/2 tsp baking powder
- 1/4 tsp salt
- 1/2 tsp ground cinnamon
- 1/4 tsp ground nutmeg
- 1/2 cup milk
- 2 large eggs
- 1/4 cup unsalted butter, melted
- 1 tsp vanilla extract
- 1/4 cup granulated sugar (for coating)
- 1 tsp ground cinnamon (for coating)

Instructions:

1. Preheat the oven to 375°F (190°C) and grease a donut pan.
2. In a large bowl, whisk together the flour, sugar, baking powder, salt, cinnamon, and nutmeg.
3. In a separate bowl, whisk together the milk, eggs, melted butter, and vanilla.
4. Add the wet ingredients to the dry ingredients and stir until just combined.
5. Spoon the batter into the donut pan, filling each mold about 2/3 full.
6. Bake for 10-12 minutes, or until a toothpick inserted comes out clean.
7. While the donuts are baking, mix the cinnamon and sugar for the coating in a small bowl.
8. Let the donuts cool for a few minutes, then toss them in the cinnamon sugar mixture.

Nutella-Stuffed Crepes
Ingredients:

- 1 cup all-purpose flour
- 2 large eggs
- 1 1/4 cups milk
- 2 tbsp unsalted butter, melted
- 1 tsp vanilla extract
- 1/4 tsp salt
- 1/2 cup Nutella
- Powdered sugar (for dusting)

Instructions:

1. In a bowl, whisk together the flour, eggs, milk, melted butter, vanilla, and salt until smooth.
2. Heat a non-stick skillet over medium heat and lightly grease with butter.
3. Pour a small amount of batter into the skillet, swirling to coat the bottom. Cook for 1-2 minutes until the edges begin to lift, then flip and cook for another 30 seconds.
4. Spread Nutella on half of the crepe, then fold it in half or roll it up.
5. Repeat with the remaining batter and Nutella.
6. Dust with powdered sugar and serve.

Cream Puffs
Ingredients:

- 1/2 cup water
- 1/2 cup unsalted butter
- 1 cup all-purpose flour
- 1/4 tsp salt
- 4 large eggs
- 1 cup heavy cream
- 2 tbsp powdered sugar
- 1 tsp vanilla extract

Instructions:

1. Preheat the oven to 400°F (200°C) and line a baking sheet with parchment paper.
2. In a saucepan, bring the water and butter to a boil. Remove from heat and stir in the flour and salt.
3. Return the pan to low heat and cook for 1-2 minutes, stirring constantly. Remove from heat and let cool slightly.
4. Beat in the eggs, one at a time, until the dough is smooth.
5. Spoon the dough onto the prepared baking sheet in small mounds. Bake for 20-25 minutes, or until golden and puffed.
6. While the cream puffs are cooling, whip the cream with powdered sugar and vanilla until stiff peaks form.
7. Cut the cooled cream puffs in half and fill with whipped cream. Serve immediately.

Maple Bacon Scones
Ingredients:

- 2 cups all-purpose flour
- 1/4 cup granulated sugar
- 1 tbsp baking powder
- 1/2 tsp salt
- 1/2 cup cold unsalted butter, cubed
- 1/2 cup cooked bacon, crumbled
- 1/4 cup maple syrup
- 1/2 cup heavy cream
- 1 large egg
- 1/2 tsp vanilla extract
- 2 tbsp maple syrup (for glaze)
- 1 tbsp powdered sugar (for glaze)

Instructions:

1. Preheat the oven to 400°F (200°C) and line a baking sheet with parchment paper.
2. In a large bowl, whisk together the flour, sugar, baking powder, and salt.
3. Cut in the cold butter using a pastry cutter or fork until the mixture resembles coarse crumbs.
4. Stir in the crumbled bacon.
5. In a separate bowl, whisk together the maple syrup, heavy cream, egg, and vanilla extract.
6. Add the wet ingredients to the dry ingredients and stir until just combined.
7. Turn the dough onto a floured surface and gently knead it into a disc about 1 inch thick. Cut into 8 wedges and place them on the prepared baking sheet.
8. Bake for 18-20 minutes, or until golden.
9. Mix the maple syrup and powdered sugar for the glaze and drizzle over the warm scones before serving.

Mocha Cake
Ingredients:

- 1 1/2 cups all-purpose flour
- 1 1/2 tsp baking powder
- 1/4 tsp salt
- 1/4 cup cocoa powder
- 1/2 cup hot brewed coffee
- 1/2 cup unsalted butter, softened
- 1 cup granulated sugar
- 2 large eggs
- 1 tsp vanilla extract
- 1/2 cup whole milk
- 1/2 cup heavy cream
- 2 oz dark chocolate, melted
- 1/4 cup powdered sugar (for frosting)

Instructions:

1. Preheat the oven to 350°F (175°C) and grease and flour two 9-inch cake pans.
2. In a medium bowl, whisk together the flour, baking powder, salt, and cocoa powder.
3. In a separate bowl, whisk together the hot coffee and cocoa powder until smooth.
4. In a large bowl, beat the softened butter and sugar until light and fluffy. Add the eggs one at a time, beating well after each addition.
5. Add the vanilla extract, followed by the milk and the coffee-cocoa mixture. Mix until combined.
6. Gradually add the dry ingredients and stir until just combined.
7. Pour the batter evenly into the prepared cake pans.
8. Bake for 25-30 minutes, or until a toothpick inserted comes out clean.
9. Let the cakes cool completely.
10. For the frosting, whip the heavy cream until stiff peaks form, then fold in the melted chocolate and powdered sugar. Frost the cooled cakes and serve.

Bourbon Pecan Pie
Ingredients:

- 1 1/2 cups pecan halves
- 1 cup granulated sugar
- 1/2 cup light corn syrup
- 1/4 cup bourbon
- 3 large eggs, beaten
- 2 tbsp unsalted butter, melted
- 1 tsp vanilla extract
- 1/4 tsp salt
- 1 9-inch pie crust (store-bought or homemade)

Instructions:

1. Preheat the oven to 350°F (175°C) and place the pie crust on a baking sheet.
2. In a large bowl, whisk together the sugar, corn syrup, bourbon, eggs, butter, vanilla extract, and salt until smooth.
3. Stir in the pecans.
4. Pour the filling into the prepared pie crust.
5. Bake for 50-60 minutes, or until the pie is set and the filling is slightly puffed.
6. Let the pie cool to room temperature before serving.

Chocolate Tart
Ingredients:

- 1 1/2 cups graham cracker crumbs
- 1/4 cup granulated sugar
- 1/2 cup unsalted butter, melted
- 1 1/2 cups heavy cream
- 8 oz dark chocolate, chopped
- 1/2 tsp vanilla extract
- Pinch of salt

Instructions:

1. Preheat the oven to 350°F (175°C).
2. In a medium bowl, combine the graham cracker crumbs, sugar, and melted butter. Press the mixture into the bottom and sides of a tart pan.
3. Bake the crust for 10-12 minutes, then remove from the oven and let cool.
4. In a saucepan, heat the heavy cream over medium heat until it just begins to simmer.
5. Pour the cream over the chopped dark chocolate and let sit for 2-3 minutes. Stir until smooth.
6. Add the vanilla extract and salt.
7. Pour the chocolate filling into the cooled tart crust and smooth the top.
8. Refrigerate for at least 2 hours before serving.

Flourless Chocolate Cake
Ingredients:

- 8 oz dark chocolate, chopped
- 1/2 cup unsalted butter
- 3/4 cup granulated sugar
- 3 large eggs, beaten
- 1 tsp vanilla extract
- 1/4 tsp salt
- Powdered sugar (for dusting)

Instructions:

1. Preheat the oven to 350°F (175°C) and grease and line an 8-inch round cake pan with parchment paper.
2. In a saucepan, melt the chocolate and butter over low heat, stirring until smooth.
3. Remove from heat and stir in the sugar, eggs, vanilla extract, and salt.
4. Pour the batter into the prepared pan and bake for 20-25 minutes, or until the cake is set and a toothpick inserted comes out clean.
5. Let the cake cool completely, then dust with powdered sugar before serving.

Marzipan Fruit Cake

Ingredients:

- 1 1/2 cups all-purpose flour
- 1 1/2 tsp baking powder
- 1/2 tsp ground cinnamon
- 1/4 tsp ground nutmeg
- 1/4 tsp ground allspice
- 1/2 cup unsalted butter, softened
- 1 cup granulated sugar
- 3 large eggs
- 1/2 cup milk
- 1/4 cup marzipan, grated
- 1/2 cup mixed dried fruit (raisins, currants, sultanas)
- 1/2 cup chopped candied peel

Instructions:

1. Preheat the oven to 325°F (165°C) and grease and line a 9-inch round cake pan.
2. In a medium bowl, whisk together the flour, baking powder, cinnamon, nutmeg, and allspice.
3. In a large bowl, cream together the butter and sugar until light and fluffy. Add the eggs one at a time, beating well after each addition.
4. Gradually add the dry ingredients, alternating with the milk. Stir in the grated marzipan, dried fruit, and candied peel.
5. Pour the batter into the prepared pan and bake for 45-50 minutes, or until a toothpick comes out clean.
6. Let the cake cool completely before serving.

Baked Donuts with Glaze
Ingredients:

- 1 1/2 cups all-purpose flour
- 1 tsp baking powder
- 1/4 tsp salt
- 1/2 tsp ground nutmeg
- 1/2 cup granulated sugar
- 2 large eggs
- 1/2 cup milk
- 1/4 cup unsalted butter, melted
- 1 tsp vanilla extract
- 1 1/2 cups powdered sugar (for glaze)
- 2 tbsp milk (for glaze)

Instructions:

1. Preheat the oven to 375°F (190°C) and grease a donut pan.
2. In a medium bowl, whisk together the flour, baking powder, salt, and nutmeg.
3. In a separate bowl, beat the sugar, eggs, milk, melted butter, and vanilla extract until smooth.
4. Stir the wet ingredients into the dry ingredients until just combined.
5. Spoon the batter into the donut pan, filling each mold about 2/3 full.
6. Bake for 10-12 minutes, or until a toothpick inserted comes out clean.
7. While the donuts are baking, mix the powdered sugar and milk for the glaze.
8. Let the donuts cool slightly before dipping them in the glaze. Serve immediately.

www.ingramcontent.com/pod-product-compliance
Lightning Source LLC
LaVergne TN
LVHW081506060526
838201LV00056BA/2961